Ruth's new family

Story by Penny Frank

Illustrated by Tony Morris

THE LION
STORY BIBLE

15

OXFORD · BATAVIA · SYDNEY

The Bible tells us
how God chose the Israelites to be his
special people. He made them a
promise that he would always love
and care for them. But they must
obey him.

This is the story of Ruth. She was
from the land of Moab, but she
wanted the God of the Israelites to be
her God too. You will find her story in
the part of the Bible which has her
name.

Copyright © 1984 Lion Publishing

Published by
Lion Publishing plc
Sandy Lane West, Littlemore, Oxford, England
ISBN 0 85648 740 6
Lion Publishing Corporation
1705 Hubbard Avenue, Batavia,
Illinois 60510, USA
ISBN 0 85648 740 6
Albatross Books Pty Ltd
PO Box 320, Sutherland, NSW 2232, Australia
ISBN 0 86760 524 3

First edition 1984
Reprinted 1984, 1985, 1988

Printed in Yugoslavia
Bound in Great Britain

**British Library Cataloguing in
Publication Data**

Frank, Penny
  Ruth's new family. - (The Lion Story
Bible; 15)
  1. Ruth - Juvenile literature
I. Title   II. Morris, Tony
222'.3509505   BS580.R8

ISBN 0-85648-740-6

**Library of Congress Cataloging in
Publication Data**

1. Ruth (Biblical character)—Juvenile
literature. 2. Bible. O.T.—Biography—
Juvenile literature. [1. Ruth (Biblical
character) 2. Bible stories—O.T.] I.
Morris, Tony, ill. II. Title. III. Series:
Frank, Penny. Lion Story Bible; 15.
BS580.R8F7 1984   222'.3509505
84-17093
ISBN 0-85648-740-6

The people of Israel were very hungry.
There had been no rain. Nothing could
grow, and when it was harvest time
there was nothing to store away.

Many Israelite families moved away
to places where there was food.

One family went to live in Moab. They
were Elimelech, his wife Naomi and
their two sons.

They were sad to leave Israel but
they worked hard in Moab to grow food
and to make friends.

As time went by they began to feel it was their home. But they never forgot Israel and their own people there.

When the two sons grew up they got
married. Their wives were very
beautiful. One was called Orpah and
the other was called Ruth.

Elimelech and Naomi were very
pleased they had such a happy family.

Then something really terrible happened. Elimelech and both his sons became ill and died.

Naomi was so sad. 'I will never manage without them,' she said.

Orpah and Ruth were sad too, but they said they would take care of Naomi.

One day Naomi had some good news
from Bethlehem, her old home.

'We have had many good harvests,'
the Israelites said. 'God is caring for us
and giving us food.'

'I would love to go back to my old home,' said Naomi. Ruth and Orpah said they would go with her.

'That is silly,' said Naomi. 'You should stay in your own land where you will be happy.'

So Orpah went back to her family, but Ruth said she really wanted to go with Naomi. Naomi tried to make her stay.

'No,' said Ruth. 'I love you so much that I will come with you. Please don't ask me to leave you. I want to belong to Israel like you, and to serve your God.'

Naomi was very happy to have Ruth
with her. So they set off for Bethlehem.

As they walked into Bethlehem they heard the people say, 'Is that really Naomi? Yes, it must be! Hello, Naomi.'

The people were glad to meet Ruth. They wanted to hear all that had happened to the family in Moab.

When at last Naomi and Ruth were living in Naomi's little house, Ruth said, 'How will we buy the food we need? We have no money.'

Naomi said, 'God will care for us.'

Naomi told Ruth that in Israel the farmers helped the poor people.

God had told them to leave enough grain in the fields and fruit on the trees for poor people to collect and eat.

So every day Ruth went to the farm
near their house.

There was plenty left when the men
had cut the harvest. Ruth went round the
field and collected grain to take
home to Naomi.

One day Boaz the farmer came to the field.

'Who is that collecting grain?' he asked his men.

'That is Ruth,' the men said. 'She is the kind girl from Moab who came back with Naomi. She is collecting food for them both to eat.'

Boaz said, 'She is kind. But it is hard for her. She needs a husband to look after her. I will talk to my cousin. He should marry her. But if he will not marry her, then I will.'

Boaz asked his cousin. He did not want to marry Ruth. So Boaz went to ask the Elders of Bethlehem if he could marry her.

'I want to marry Ruth from Moab,' he said. 'I will look after her so that she won't have to do this hard work. We will be able to take care of Naomi together.'

The Elders said it was a splendid idea.

Boaz and Ruth got married. It was very exciting. The whole town of Bethlehem was there. Ruth did not have to work in the fields now. She and Naomi had plenty to eat.

Boaz and Ruth had a very happy home
to share with Naomi. Soon Ruth had a
baby boy.

   'Now we are completely happy,'
they said.

   Naomi smiled and held the baby
close.

They thanked God for all he had given
them.

Ruth and Naomi said, 'Thank you for
bringing us back to Bethlehem.'

Boaz said, 'Thank you for my
family.'

They all said, 'Thank you for the new baby.'

That baby, Obed, grew up to be the grandfather of King David. And from David's family another king was born many years later. His name was Jesus.

The Lion Story Bible is made up of 52 individual stories for young readers, building up an understanding of the Bible as one story–God's story–a story for all time and all people.

The Old Testament section (numbers 1-30) tells the story of a great nation–God's chosen people, the Israelites–and God's love and care for them through good times and bad. The stories are about people who knew and trusted God. From this nation came one special person, Jesus Christ, sent by God to save all people everywhere.

Ruth's new family comes from the Old Testament book of Ruth. Only four chapters long, it is one of the gems of the Bible. Ruth was not an Israelite. She was a foreigner from Moab, on the far side of the Dead Sea. But such was her love for Naomi that she left her own country and her family to return with Naomi to Bethlehem: 'Let your people be my people, your God my God.'

The story makes it plain that God loves all who will follow him, whatever their race. He not only provided for the needs of Ruth and Naomi, he chose Ruth to begin the family from which King David of Israel and eventually Jesus himself was born.

The next book in the series, number 16: *God speaks to Samuel,* is the familiar and much-loved story of the birth and boyhood of Samuel, one of Israel's greatest leaders.